I AM WORTH THE WAIT

COLORING BOOK

a children's book that promotes positive
self-esteem, self-worth and self-confidence

BY: LINDSAY M. WARREN, MD

Order this book online at www.trafford.com
or email orders@trafford.com

Most Trafford titles are also available at major online book retailers.

Print information available on the last page.

ISBN: 978-1-6987-0496-8 (sc)
ISBN: 978-1-6987-0493-7 (hc)
ISBN: 978-1-6987-0494-4 (e)

Library of Congress Control Number: 2020924445

Trafford rev. 03/05/2021

Trafford PUBLISHING® www.trafford.com
North America & international
toll-free: 844-688-6899 (USA & Canada)
fax: 812 355 4082

This book is dedicated to
my sweet girls, **Grace,
Charis and Hannah**. Daddy
and I love you very much.
Each one of you is a special
treasure from God!!

I would like to give special thanks to **Whitney Tarver** (my sister), **Elice Browne** (my sister in Christ) and **Gareth Warren** (my husband). Your collective assistance with this children's book has been so helpful. I appreciate your insight and attention to detail.

Mommy and Daddy always share encouraging words with me. They build my self-esteem and help me to understand my worth and value.

Mommy says, I am Awesome...

Daddy says, I am Brilliant...

Mommy says, I am Creative...

Daddy says, I am Delightful...

Mommy says, I am Excellent...

Daddy says, I am Fearless...

Mommy says, I am Gifted...

Daddy says, I am Helpful...

Mommy says, I am Intelligent...

Daddy says, I am Joyful...

Mommy says, I am Kind...

Daddy says, I am Loved...

Mommy says, I am Marvelous...

Daddy says, I am Nice...

Mommy says, I am

Outstanding...

Daddy says, I am Precious...

Mommy says, I am Quite clever...

Daddy says, I am Rare...

Mommy says, I am Special...

Daddy says, I am Talented...

Mommy says, I am Unique...

Daddy says, I am Very polite...

Mommy says, I am Wonderful...

Daddy says, I am eXquisite...

Mommy says, I am

extraordinar Y ...

Z

Daddy says, I am amaZing...

And, God say, **I AM A GREAT TREASURE** that is loved by Him and...

I AM WORTH THE WAIT!!!

Printed in the United States
by Baker & Taylor Publisher Services